Eco-Cities

New Healthy Architecture

© 2021 Monsa Publications

First edition in 2021 November by Monsa Publications,
Gravina 43 (08930) Sant Adrià de Besós.
Barcelona (Spain)
T +34 93 381 00 93
www.monsa.com monsa@monsa.com

Project director Anna Minguet.
Art director & Layout Eva Minguet.
(Monsa Publications)

Printed in Spain by Cachiman Gráfic.
Translation by SomosTraductores.

Image on page 2-3 and 142-143 courtesy of ADNBA.

Shop online:
www.monsashop.com

Follow us!
Instagram @monsapublications
Facebook @monsashop

ISBN 978-84-17557-41-6
D.L. B 17121-2021

Eco-Cities

New Healthy Architecture

monsa

INTRODUCTION

The creation of pleasant living environments that avoid the simple container of human beings and build spaces of coexistence receptive to the needs of users has been one of the objectives of architectural practice for decades.

The projects presented in this book are magnificent recent examples of how architecture can create attractive residential buildings aware of their social function, promoting interaction between users and the harmonious relationship of the community with its natural and urban environment. Likewise, all of them transmit a great sensitivity towards issues such as sustainability, eco efficiency or the integration and conservation of historical and industrial heritage, using construction methods ranging from traditional techniques to the most modern parametric design systems.

La creación de entornos habitables agradables que construyan espacios de convivencia receptivos a las necesidades de los usuarios ha constituido desde hace décadas uno de los objetivos de la práctica arquitectónica.

Los proyectos presentados en este libro son magníficos ejemplos recientes de cómo la arquitectura puede crear atractivos edificios de viviendas conscientes de su función social, promoviendo la interacción entre los usuarios y la relación armoniosa de la comunidad con su entorno natural y urbano. Así mismo, todos ellos transmiten una gran sensibilidad hacia temas como la sostenibilidad, la ecoeficiencia o la integración y conservación del patrimonio histórico e industrial, utilizando para ello métodos constructivos que van desde las técnicas tradicionales hasta los más modernos sistemas de diseño paramétrico.

PROJECTS

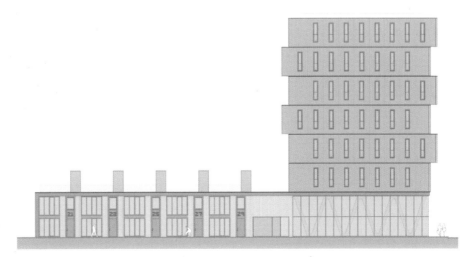

ARCHITEKTI ŠEBO LICHÝ

RESIDENTIAL BUILDING NOVÝ HÁJ

Bratislava, Slovakia
www.sebolichy.sk

The architectural concept of Nový háj is based on two essential factors:
Firstly, a direct reaction to its location in Petržalka, the largest housing complex of precast concrete panels in Central Europe, which is a relic of the communist era. The building's two towers make the most of their visual contact with the nearby woods and park, and each apartment is facing two façades.
The second factor is the active participation of the residents in the architectural conception of the building. Its flexible design and the architectural language used allow clients to choose the size and location of their windows and balconies without compromising the coherence of the whole. The result of this approach is an authentic architecture that reflects the real life of real people.

El concepto arquitectónico de Nový háj se basa en dos factores esenciales:
En primer lugar, una reacción directa frente a su ubicación en Petržalka, el mayor conjunto de viviendas de paneles prefabricados de hormigón en Europa Central, que constituye una reliquia de la era comunista. Las dos torres del edificio sacan el máximo provecho de su contacto visual con los bosques y el parque cercanos, y cada apartamento goza de orientación hacia dos fachadas. El segundo factor es la participación activa de los residentes en la concepción arquitectónica del edificio. Su diseño flexible y el lenguaje arquitectónico empleado permiten que los clientes puedan elegir el tamaño y la ubicación de sus ventanas y balcones sin comprimeter la coherencia del conjunto. El resultado de este enfoque es una arquitectura auténtica que refleja la vida real de personas reales en su interior.

Architect: Mgr. arch. Igor Lichý, Ing. arch. Tomáš Šebo,
Ing. arch. Drahan Petrovic,
Ing. arch. Katarína Uhnáková,
Ing. arch. Emanuel Zatlukaj.
Investor: ITB Development and Imagine Development
General contractor: Me&Co
Statics: Konstrukt+
Land area: 2,206 m2
Utility area: 6,504.51 m2
Building area: 1,868 m2
Building volume: 25,750 m3
Nº of flats: 75
General contractor: Me&Co
Photo credits: © Dano Veselský, © Olja Triaska Stefanovic, © Lubo Stacho
Awards: Slovak Apartment Block

10

Site plan

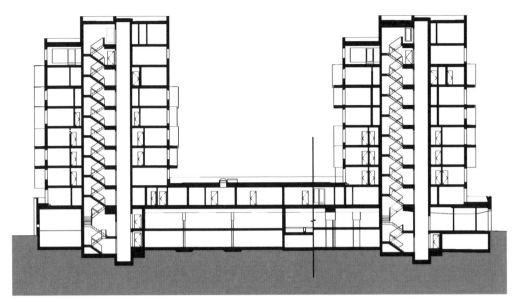

Section

North elevation

Windows and loggias position before client's changes

Windows and loggias position after client's changes

East elevation

Windows and loggias position before client's changes

Windows and loggias position after client's changes

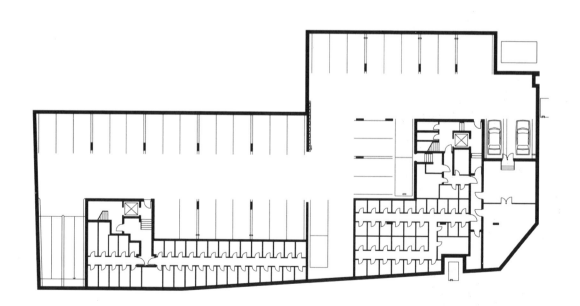

Lower ground floor plan

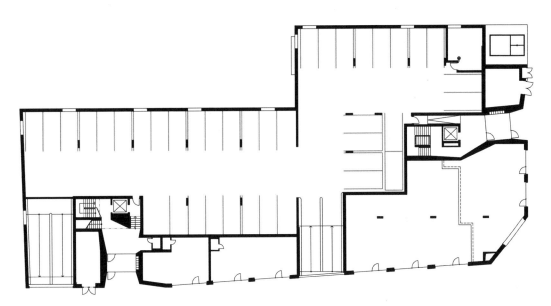

Ground floor plan

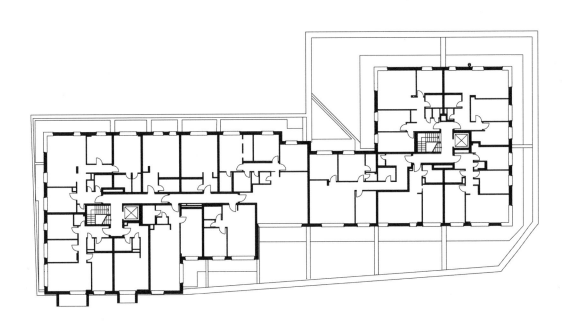

First floor plan

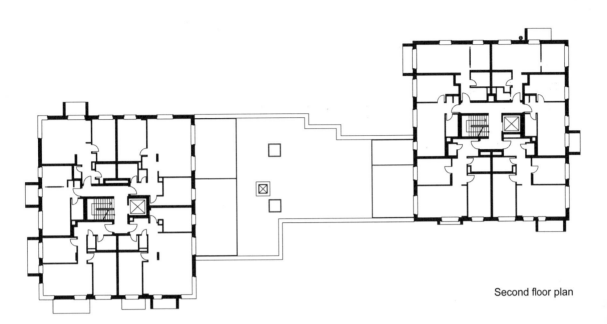

Second floor plan

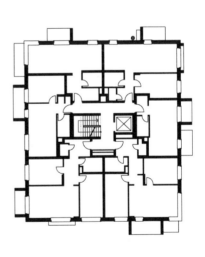

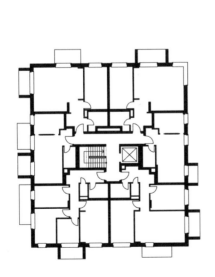

Third floor plan

ADNBA
URBAN SPACES
1'/DOGARILOR 26-30 HOUSING
Bucarest, Romania
www.adnba.ro

In response to the densification of the central area of
Bucharest, the project tries to integrate into a puzzle of
new and old buildings of different typologies and scales.
The intervention, structured in two volumes, seeks to
reproduce the porosity and depth of the plots in the area
and attempts to capture part of the collage aspect of the
surroundings. The exterior volume has a permeable ground
floor that opens the building towards the street and a
façade that mediates between the alignment required
by municipal regulations and the fragmentation of the
surrounding urban fabric.
The 77 residential units that make up the project are of
different sizes and typologies and are designed with a
flexibility that allows two or more units to be connected
horizontally or vertically. The apartments are complemented
with several exterior and interior common spaces.

Como respuesta a la densificación del área central de Bucarest,
el proyecto trata de integrarse en un rompecabezas de
edificios nuevos y antiguos de diferentes tipologías y escalas.
La intervención, estructurada en dos volúmenes, busca
reproducir la porosidad y la profundidad de las parcelas de
la zona e intenta capturar parte del aspecto de "collage" de
los alrededores. El volumen exterior tiene una planta baja
permeable que abre el edificio hacia la calle y una fachada
que media entre la alineación requerida por la normativa
municipal y la fragmentación del tejido urbano circundante.
Las 77 unidades residenciales que componen el proyecto son
de diferentes tamaños y tipologías y están diseñadas con una
flexibilidad que permite conectar horizontal o verticalmente
dos o más unidades. Los apartamentos se complementan con
varios espacios comunes exteriores e interiores.

Place: 17bis, Dr. Grigore Mora Street, Bucharest, Romania
Architecture and design coordination: ADNBA
Developer: Private
Project management: Epstein PM&Consulting
Authors: Adrian Untaru, Andrei S, erbescu, Bogdan Braˇdaˇt,eanu, Marius
Dumitras,cu, Ruxandra Bardas,Carmen Petrea
Photo credits: © Cosmin Dragomir
Number of units: 5 apartments
Total built area: 2,020 m2
Awards:
- Mies van der Rohe Awards, nominated
- National Biennale of Architecture Bucharest, Housing category, nominated

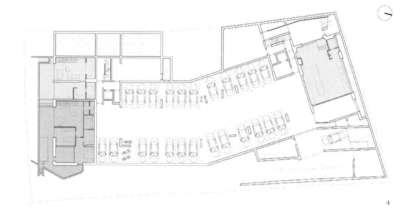

Basement floor plan

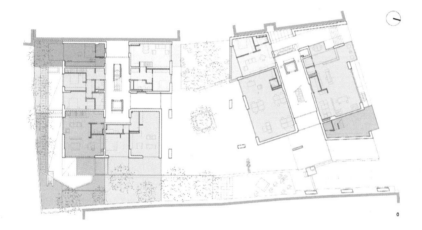

Ground floor plan

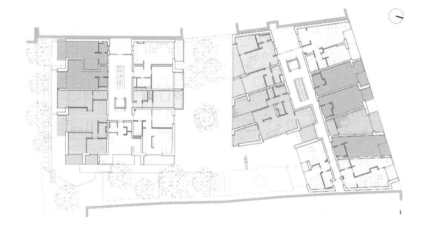

First floor plan

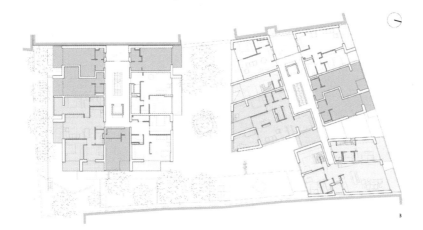

Third floor plan

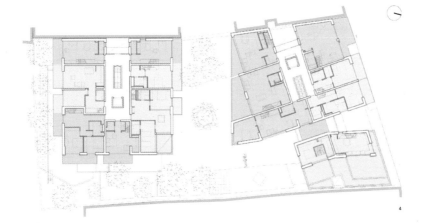

Fourth floor plan

Site plan

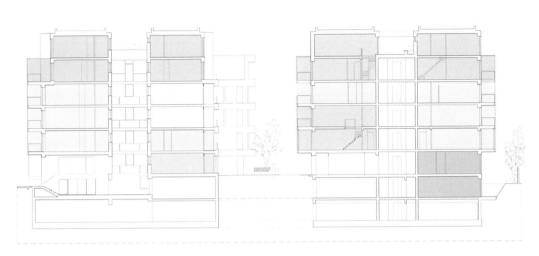

Building section

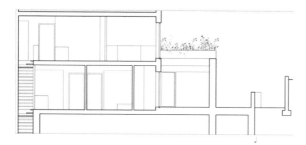

Duplex apartment. Section

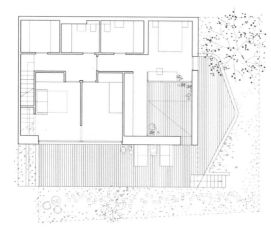

Duplex apartment. First floor

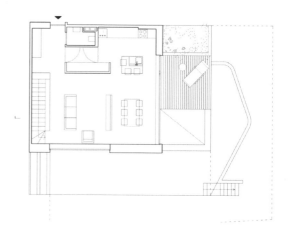

Duplex apartment. Ground floor

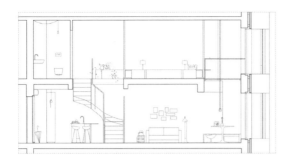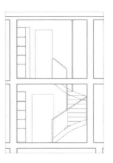

Duplex apartment. Section

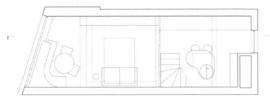

Duplex apartment. First floor

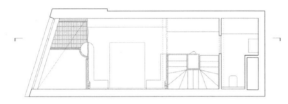

Duplex apartment. Ground floor

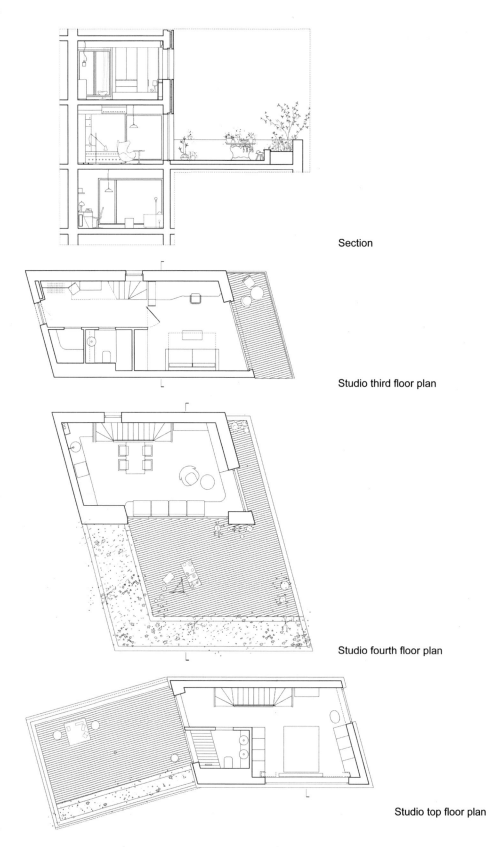

Section

Studio third floor plan

Studio fourth floor plan

Studio top floor plan

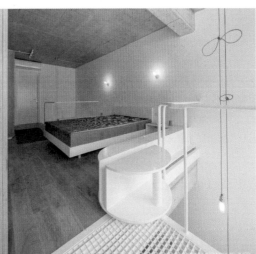

BOGEVISCHS BUERO

COOPERATIVE HOUSING COMPLEX WAGNISART
Munich, Germany
www.bogevisch.de

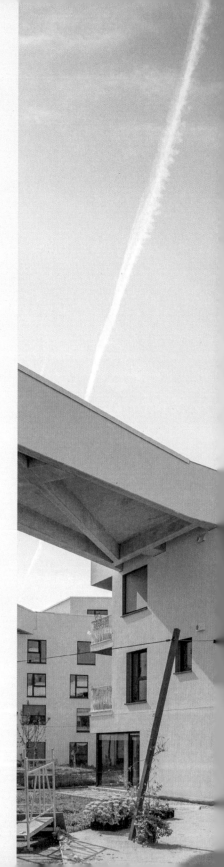

The project is located in the district of Domagkpark and was developed together with its future inhabitants. The planning allowed few restrictions on the design of the buildings and placed them around patios and passages forming open communal spaces.
The complex consists of five buildings, the upper floors of which are connected to each other by bridges that create a unique landscape of elevated gardens. The ground floors house community rooms, workshops, offices and open spaces for the activities of residents and the neighbourhood.
wagnisART is a certified passive building with heat recovery ventilation, built with a hybrid system of reinforced concrete load-bearing walls and a suspended timber façade. The reduction in parking space due to a mobility concept underlines the sustainability of the project.

El proyecto se sitúa en el distrito de Domagkpark y fue desarrollado conjuntamente con sus futuros habitantes. El planeamiento permitió pocas restricciones en el diseño de los edificios y situarlos alrededor de patios y pasajes formando espacios comunitarios abiertos al entorno.
El complejo consta de cinco edificios, cuyas plantas superiores se conectan entre sí a través de puentes generadores de un paisaje único de jardines elevados. Las plantas bajas albergan salas comunitarias, talleres, oficinas y espacios abiertos, destinados a las actividades de los residentes y del vecindario.
wagnisART es un edificio pasivo certificado con ventilación de recuperación de calor, construido con un sistema híbrido de muros de carga hormigón armado y fachada suspendida. La reducción del espacio de estacionamiento por un concepto de movilidad subraya la sostenibilidad del proyecto.

Name of the client: Wohnbaugenossenschaft wagnis eG
Name of the architect:
Joint venture bogevischs buero architekten & stadtplaner GmbH / SHAG Schindler Hable Architekten GbR (design stages 1-5)
Design stages 6-9: SHAG Schindler Hable Architekten GbR with Architekturbüro Christian Köhler
Net floor area: 9,590 m²/ 138 Appartments
Energy performance certificate rating: Passive House
Building area (m2): 20,275 m²
Photo credits: © Michael Heinrich, Munich
Awards:
- "Ehrenpreis für guten Wohnungsbau" der Stadt München
- "Honorable Award" of the City of Munich
- The DAM (Deutsches Architektur Museum) Award for Architecture in Germany
- Award of the DGNB (German Sustainable Building Council)
- Prize Sustainable Building
- Nominated for the "Deutscher Bauherrenpreis"
- Awarded with the "Deutscher Städtebaupreis"
- Award of the "Deutscher Landschaftsarchitektur-Preis"

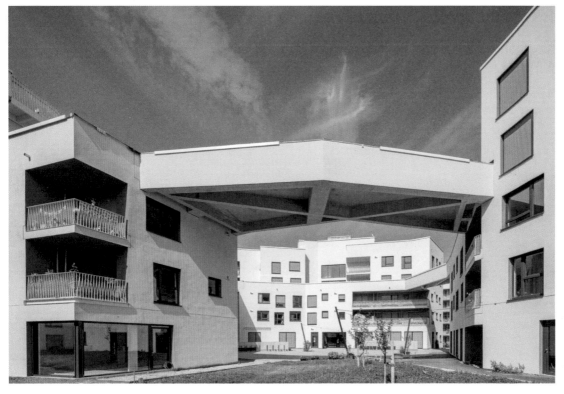

Location map

Site plan

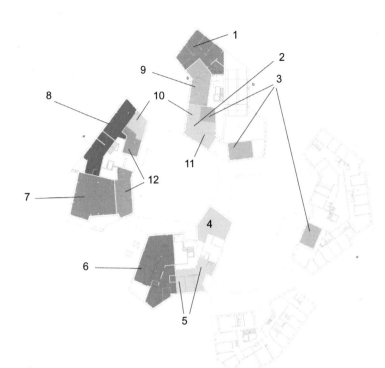

Ground floor plan

1. Office spaces
2. Common laundry
3. Bicycle and buggy room
4. Community room
5. Guest apartments
6. Café
7. Event space
8. Medical treatment rooms
9. Workshops
10. Community studio
11. Common sewing room
12. Artist studios

Type floor plan

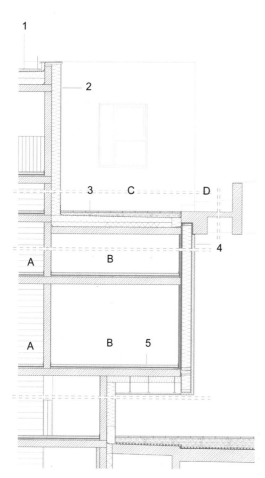

Facade section

A. Stairwell
B. Apartment
C. Roof terrace
D. Bridge

1. Roof construction
- 40 mm grit
- 5 mm protection mat
- 5 mm 2nd layer of bitumen seal
- 3 mm 1st layer of bitumen seal
- 300 mm (on average) gradient insulation
- 3 mm vapor barrier
- 220 mm reinforced concrete

2. Constructionofexteriorwall reinforced concrete
- 15 mm plaster
- 280 mm mineral insulation
- 10 mm glue
- 220 mm reinforced concrete
- 15 mm plaster

3. Construction of roof terrace
- 50 mm factory flagstone, concrete
- 40 mm grit 5 mm protection mat
- 5 mm 2nd layer of bitumen seal
- 3 mm 1st layer of bitumen seal
- 300 mm (on average) gradient insulation
- 3 mm vapor barrier
- 220 mm reinforced concrete

4. Constructionofexteriorwalltimber frame
- 15 mm plaster
- 60 mm mineral insulation
- 5 mm glue
- 30 mm 2 layers of gypsum fiber board as fire protection
- 300 mm timber frame, infill mineral insulation
- 30 mm 2 layers of gypsum fiber board as fire protection
- 0,5 mm vapor barrier
- 60 mm installation layer, infill mineral insulation
- 25 mm 2 layers of plaster board

5. Floor construction
- 10mm parquet
- 50 mm cement screed
- 0,2 mm PE film
- 20 mm impact sound insulation
- 60 mm EPS insulation, compensation layer
- 0,2 mm PE film
- 220 mm reinforced concrete
- 200 mm mineral insulation
- 335 mm ceiling substructure
- 10 mm fiber cement board
- 15 mm plaster

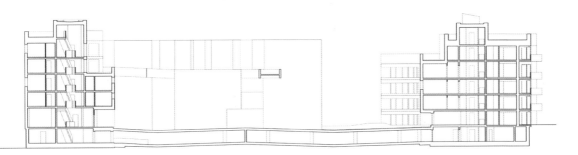

Section A-A

Transversal section

FRANTZEN ET AL ARCHITECTEN

PATCH22

Amsterdam, the Netherlands
www.groupwork.uk.com

Patch 22 is a sustainable building thanks to its energy efficiency, the use of renewable materials and the great functional flexibility offered by its design. The structure and facades are built with timber and the 4m high levels can be functionally reconverted without affecting the structure or the facilities, that are diverted to the central core. The floors enter and leave the façade plane in a playful way and can be distributed as lofts of up to 540 m2 with large balconies, as eight smaller apartments or as an open office space that occupies the entire floor thanks to the lack of structural division. All apartment layouts are custom designed for their owners. The building is equipped with multiple sustainable measures, such as a roof full of photovoltaic panels, the reuse of rainwater or the CO_2 neutral generation of heat through pellet boilers.

Patch 22 es un edificio sostenible gracias a su eficiencia energética, el uso de materiales renovables y la gran flexibilidad funcional que ofrece su diseño. Su estructura y sus fachadas están construidas con madera y sus plantas, de 4 m de altura libre, pueden reconvertir su uso y su distribución sin afectar a la estructura ni a las instalaciones, desviadas horizontalmente hacia un núcleo central. Las plantas entran y salen del plano de fachada de forma lúdica y se pueden distribuir como lofts de hasta 540 m2 con grandes balcones, como ocho apartamentos más pequeños o como espacio de oficina abierto que ocupa toda la planta gracias a la falta de división estructural. Todas las plantas de los apartamentos son diseñadas a la medida de sus propietarios. El edificio está dotado de múltiples medidas sostenibles, como una cubierta llena de paneles fotovoltaicos, la reutilización de agua de lluvia o la generación de calor mediante calderas de pellets.

Program: work-living housing
Location: Amsterdam
Partner in charge: Tom Frantzen
Team: Karel van Eijken, Laura Reinders
Client: Lemniskade Projects
(Tom Frantzen & Claus Oussoren)
Contractor: Hillen & Roosen
Gross floor area: 5,209 m2
Lettable floor area: 4,295 m2
Photo credits: © Luuk Kramer, © Isabel Nabuurs
Awards:
- First prize Golden Pyramid
- First prize "Sustainable Building Award 2018", The Dutch Sustainable Building Awards
- First prize 'WAN residential awards
- "Green Good Design Award", The European Centre for Architecture Art Design and Urban Studies
  and The Chicago Athenaeum
- Honourable mention "BNA building of the Year"
- Nomination "Amsterdamse Nieuwbouw Prijs"
- Nomination Amsterdam Architecture Prize
- Nomination 'Zuiderkerkprijs; the best housing block of Amsterdam
- Nomination ARC16 innovation award PATCH22, Amsterdam

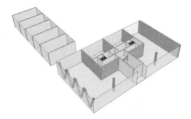

Concrete ground floor structure

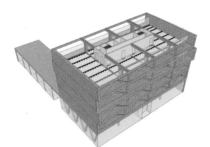

Prefab timber and concrete components

Concrete 1st floor

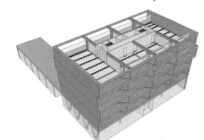

Dry-wall division walls

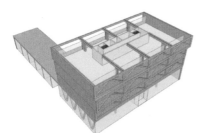

Hybrid timber / concrete / steel structure

Custom made installations inside apartments

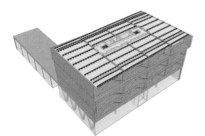

Slimline steel- concrete flooring system

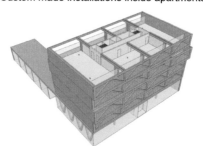

Top floors inside apartments

Structure and installations

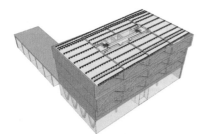

Installations in central core

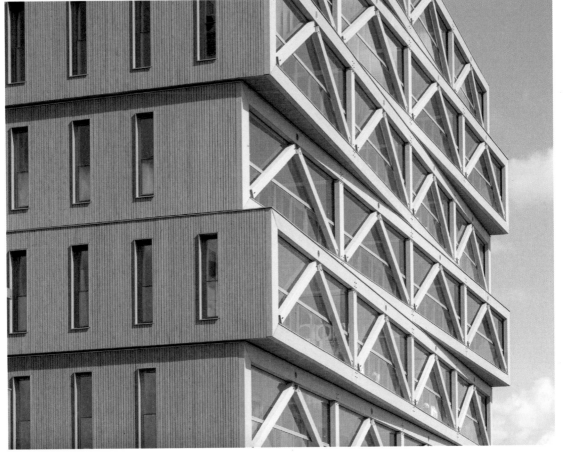

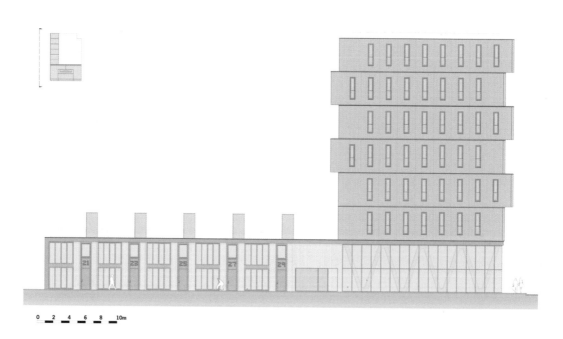

0 2 4 6 8 10m

West elevation

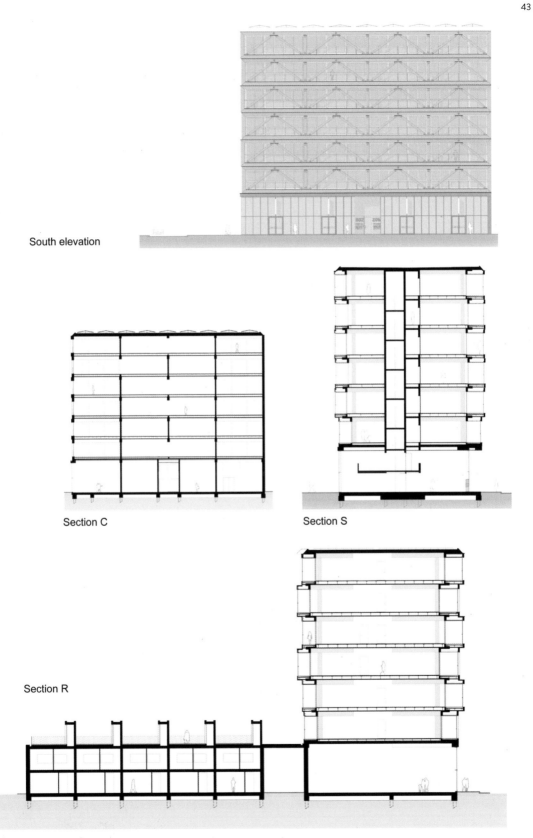

South elevation

Section C

Section S

Section R

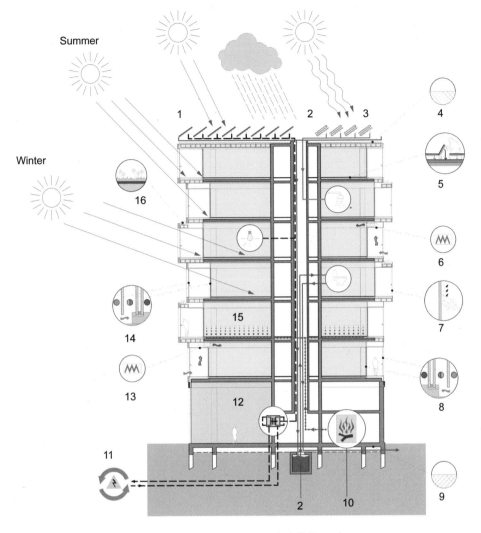

Summer

Winter

Installation scheme

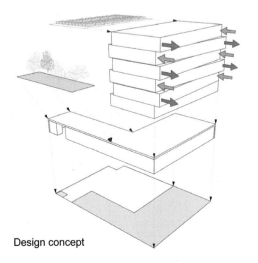

Design concept

1. Solar cells
2. Rainwater collection
3. Solar collectors
4. Insulation thermal resistance value=7
5. Removable underfloor heating panels for access to pipework and cabling
6. Heat exchanger unit
7. Single glazing noise barrier
8. Climate-protected loggia with single + double glazing
9. Insulation thermal resistance value=5
10. Pellet stove
11. Surplus electricity is stored in electricity grid
12. Transformer
13. Heat exchanger unit
14. Climate-protected loggia with single + double glazing
15. Underfloor heating
16. Sedum roof covering

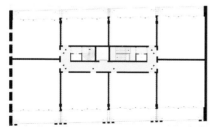

Typical floorplan

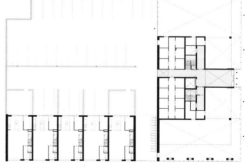

Ground floor plan

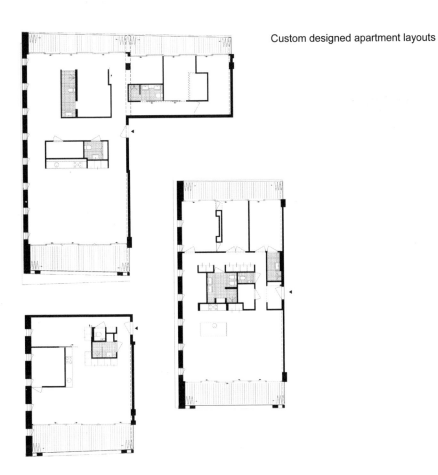

Custom designed apartment layouts

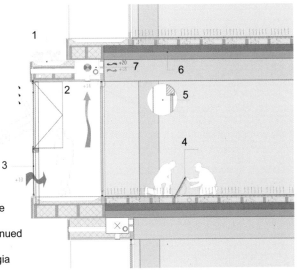

Section concept

1. Low-maintenance sedum roof
2. Glass can be opened for cleaning from the inside
3. Rear facade with soundproofed single glazing
4. Removable underfloor heating tiles ensure continued access to pipework and cabling
5. Insulating double glazing + single glazing in loggia
6. Slimline hollow floor
7. CO_2 controlled heat recovery unit

GROUPWORK

BARRETTS GROVE

London, United Kingdom
www.frantzen.nl

Barretts Grove is located in Stoke Newington and accommodates six flats on a small brownfield garage workshop site. Set between a Victorian terrace and Edwardian redbrick school it echoes the tall gables of the school and standalone 'villa' architype of the Victorian terrace. Built from cross laminated timber the structure is left exposed internally allowing its material finish to drive the character of the architecture, with the exterior using brick as an expressed nonstructural but protective perforated screen. Large wicker screened balconies are offset in elevation to allow residents to communicate with neighbours above and below.

Situado en una típica calle victoriana de casas adosadas de ladrillo, la composición exterior de este edificio de 6 apartamentos se hace eco de las dos edificaciones que lo rodean. Una pantalla perforada de ladrillo rojo recubre todo el conjunto, incluida la cubierta, expresando su naturaleza protectora pero no estructural. La retícula de grandes aberturas de las fachadas subraya la fortaleza de la forma a pesar de su esbeltez. Los largos balcones de malla de mimbre que cuelgan de las aberturas a la calle se disponen de forma alterna creando un espacio de relación social entre los vecinos de diferentes plantas. La superestructura de madera laminada cruzada con juntas de construcción visibles utilizada para levantar el edificio se deja expuesta en el interior y se hace presente también en los detalles a escala doméstica, impulsando el carácter de la arquitectura.

Gross internal floor area: 635 sqm GIA
Form of contract or procurement route: JCT Design+Build
Construction cost: £ 1.27 m
Construction cost per m2: £1,983 /m2
Architect groupwork: Dale Elliott (Project Architect), Sam Douek (Assistant Architect), Nerissa Yeung (Assistant Architect), Amin Taha (Senior Architect)
Executive architect: GROUPWORK
Client: Cobstar Developments
Project manager: GROUPWORK
CDM coordinator: Syntegra
Approved building inspector: MLM
Main contractor: Ecore Construction Ltd
Cad software used: Mixed
Annual Co2 emissions: 16.84 kg/m2
Photo credits: © Timothy Soar

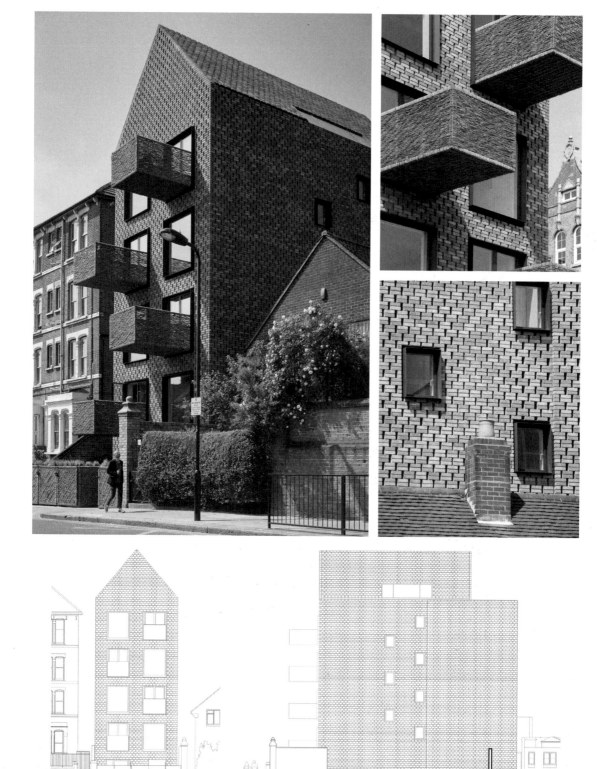

Elevations

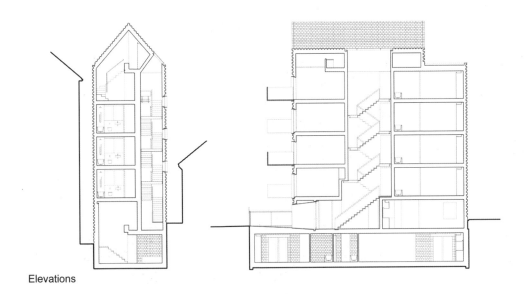

Elevations

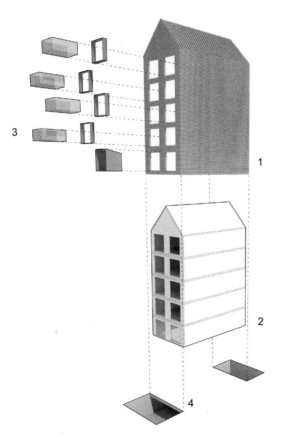

Exploded axonometry

1. Perforated brick cladding
2. Cross laminated timber structure
3. Wicker balconies
4. Light wells

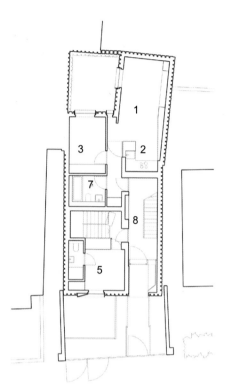

Basement plan. Unit 1

Ground floor plan. Unit 1 / 2

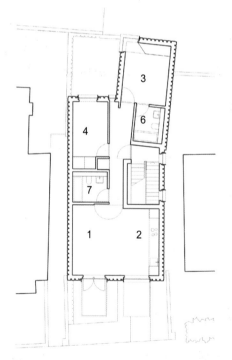

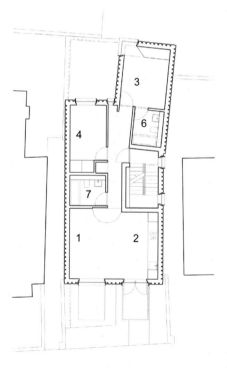

First floor plan. Unit 3

Second floor plan. Unit 4

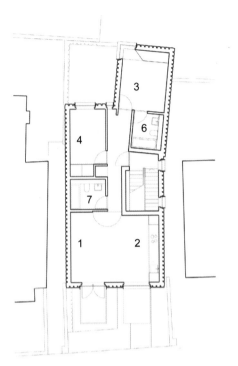

Third floor plan. Unit 5

Fourth floor main plan. Unit 6

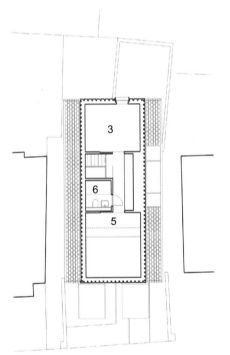

Fourth floor mezzanine plan. Unit 6

1. Living room
2. Kitchen
3. Master bedroom
4. Bedroom 2
5. Bedroom 3 / study
6. En suite
7. Bathroom
8. Entry lobby

NERMA LINSBERGER

MÜHLGRUND
Vienna, Austria
www.nermalinsberger.com

The introverted structure of this group of social dwellings is a response to its heterogeneous environment. The project defines clear boundaries on the north, east and west sides, whose façades dialogue with the surrounding urban space, and opens up towards the wide south-facing spaces. The dynamic modular structure used accommodates different types of housing, compact and with great use of space. The project promotes social interaction through the design of elements such as porticoes, staircases or connecting corridors and through community spaces, gardens and patios that strengthen the residents' sense of identification with their housing complex. Accommodation of disadvantaged social groups in the supervised housing apartments on the ground floor seeks to establish stronger community bonds and reduce prejudice.

La estructura introvertida de este conjunto de viviendas sociales es una respuesta a su entorno heterogéneo. El proyecto define unos límites claros en los lados norte, este y oeste, cuyas fachadas dialogan con el espacio urbano circundante, y se abre hacia los amplios espacios orientados a sur. La dinámica estructura modular utilizada acomoda diversas tipologías de vivienda, compactas y con gran aprovechamiento del espacio. El proyecto fomenta la interacción social a través del diseño de elementos como pórticos, escaleras o pasillos de conexión y a través de espacios comunitarios, jardines y patios que fortalecen el sentido de identificación de los residentes con su complejo de viviendas. El alojamiento de grupos sociales desfavorecidos en los apartamentos de vivienda tutelada de la planta baja busca establecer vínculos comunitarios más sólidos y reducir los prejuicios.

Type: Social housing
Location: Vienna, Austria
Floor space: 11,000 m²
Status: On site
Photo credits:
© Thomas Hennerbichler,
© Daniel Hawelka
Awards:
- Schorsch (Vienna)
M GRUND Social Housing Mühlgrund
- Architizer A+ Award Finalist (New York, USA) – M GRUND Social Housing Mühgrund
- AAP American Architecture Prize (New York, USA) M GRUND Social Housing Mühlgrund
- Best architects 19 (Düsseldorf, Germany) - M grund Social Housing Mühlgrund
- German Design Award for M GRUND Social Housing Mühlgrund
- If Design Award

58

Ground floor plan

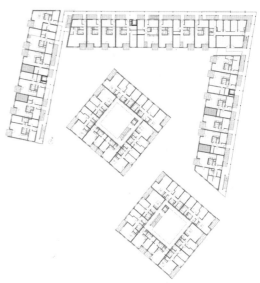

First floor plan

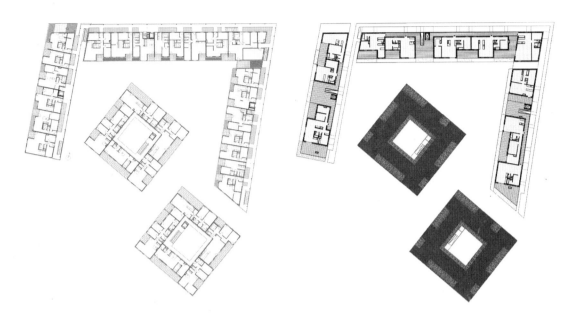

First attic floor plan
Second attic floor plan

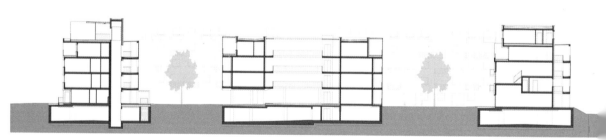

Section

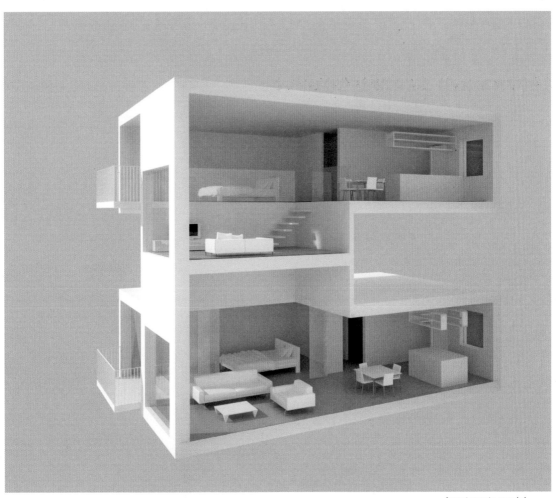

Apartments model

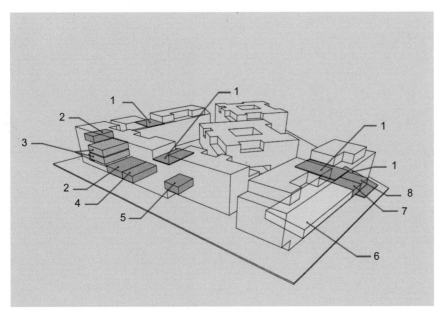

Community sketches

1. Community terrace
2. Community room
3. Zumietbare ateliers
4. Laundry
5. Workshop
6. Supervised flat share
7. Community kitchen
8. Children's playroom

OLGOO
ZAFERANIYE GARDEN COMPLEX
Tehran, Iran
www.olgooco.com

This 64-unit residential complex located in a 6500 m2 garden in northern Tehran promotes interaction between nature and city life. The footprint of the building tries to preserve the existing vegetation and the composition of its façade, based on a volumetric game with wooden boxes from 2 to 5 floors high, creates terraces with trees and plants that create microclimates and provide privacy to the houses. A rainwater recovery system allows the abundant development of this vegetation on the balconies and on the communal roof, which also includes a viewpoint, an orchard and a meeting area. The project avoids repeating the compositional schemes of the neighbouring height typologies and confers on the green layer of vegetation the range of main material of the façade, which it endows with a dynamic appearance.

Este complejo residencial de 64 viviendas ubicado en un jardín de 6.500 m2 de la zona norte de Teherán promueve la interacción entre la naturaleza y la vida de la ciudad. La huella del edificio intenta preservar la vegetación existente y la composición de su fachada, basada en un juego volúmetrico con cajas de madera de 2 a 5 pisos de altura, crea terrazas con árboles y plantas que crean microclimas y aportan privacidad a las viviendas. Un sistema de recuperación de agua de lluvia permite el desarrollo abundante de esta vegetación en los balcones y en la cubierta comunitaria, que incluye también un mirador, un huerto y una zona de reunión. El proyecto evita repetir los esquemas compositivos de las tipologías en altura vecinas y confiere a la capa verde de la vegetación el rango de material principal de la fachada, a la que dota de un aspecto dinámico.

Architect's firm: Olgoo Office
Contact e-mail: mehrankhoshroo@yahoo.com
Lead architects:
Mehran Khoshroo
Gross built area: 38,000m2
Function: Residential
Site area (plottage): 6,400 m2
Covered area: 38,000 m2
Total floor area (=gross area): 1,950 m2
Photo credits:
© Mohammad Hassan Ettefagh
Design team:
Almara Melkomian, Mehdi Atashbar, Amir Masoud Nafisi, Adel Ataei, Soudabe Qorbani, Nastaran Namvar, Tannaz Khoshroo, Ni-loofar Esmaeili, Reyhane Miraftab, Sepide Ghabelzede, Amir Hossein Mohebi, Torang Asadi, Hashem Karimi

Access and landscape

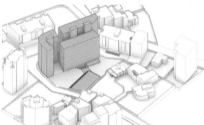

Occupation

Excavation

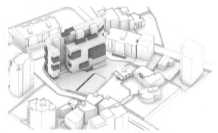

Primitive mass

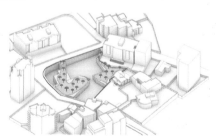

Extrusion

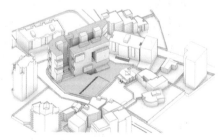

Outdoor living

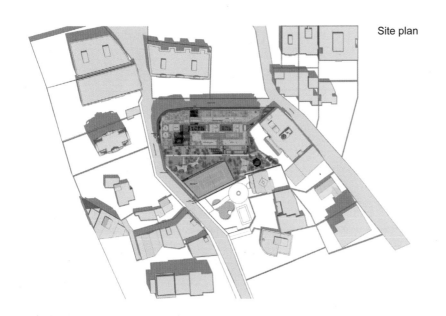

Site plan

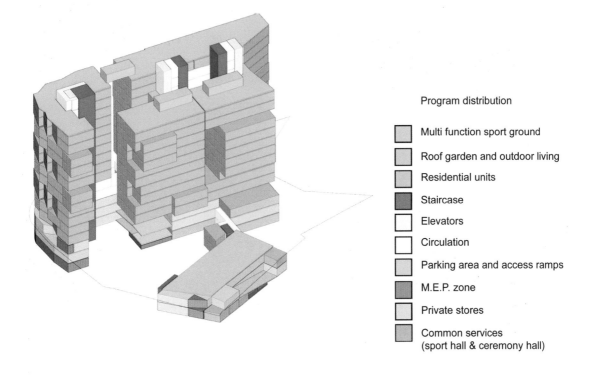

Program distribution

Multi function sport ground

Roof garden and outdoor living

Residential units

Staircase

Elevators

Circulation

Parking area and access ramps

M.E.P. zone

Private stores

Common services
(sport hall & ceremony hall)

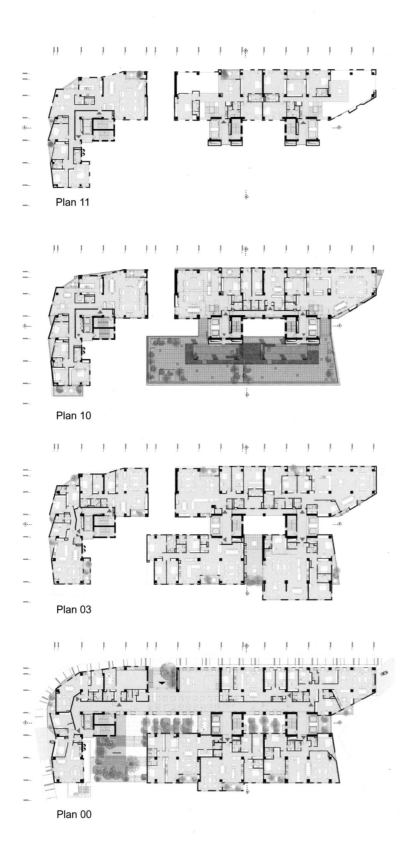

Plan 11

Plan 10

Plan 03

Plan 00

East elevation

West elevation

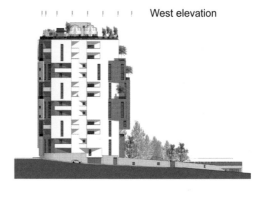

South elevation

North elevation

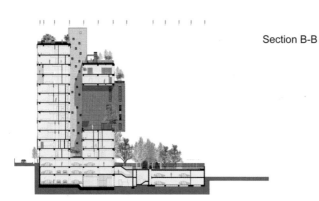

Section B-B

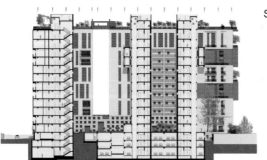

Section A-A

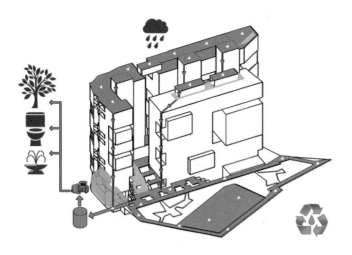

Rainwater recycling diagram

1. Green plants
2. Toilets
3. Water surface
4. Plumbing
5. Water tank

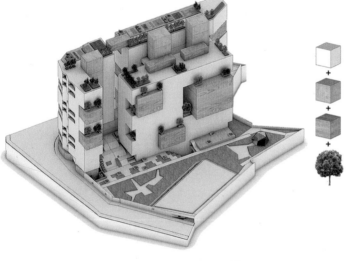

Materials

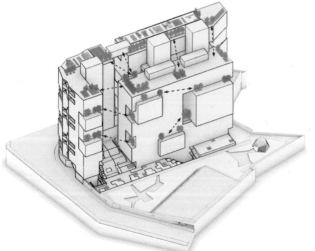

Privacy and green layer

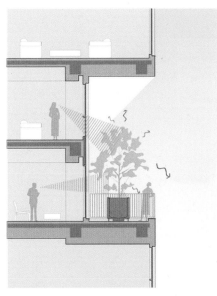

Green balconies diagram

1. In
2. Out
3. Microclimate condition around the tree
4. Min height of soil 90 cm.

RH +
ARCHITECTURE
PLEIN SOLEIL
France, Paris
www.rhplus-architecture.com

Located in a block near the bassin de la Villette, the building integrates 28 apartments and a nursery located on the ground floor. Its long main façade takes advantage of the southern orientation through a design based on galleries that regulate the temperature in the summer and winter months. These external damping spaces are closed with sliding glass panels that allow the sun's heat to be absorbed during the day and released at night. In colder climates, air from mechanical ventilation is preheated.
The apartments consist of a north-facing entrance, kitchen and bathroom, and south-facing bedrooms and living rooms with galleries. Some floors contain double-height living rooms. The western part of the building is developed in a staggered shape that generates private terraces and green roofs with views.

Situado en una manzana cercana al bassin de la Villette, el edificio integra 28 apartamentos y una guardería situada en planta baja. Su larga fachada principal aprovecha la orientación sur mediante un diseño basado en galerías que regulan la temperatura en los meses de verano e invierno. Estos espacios de amortiguación exterior se cierran con paneles correderos de vidrio que permiten que el calor del sol sea absorbido durante el día y liberado por la noche. Con clima más frío, el aire procedente de la ventilación mecánica es precalentado.
Los apartamentos constan de entrada, cocina y baño, orientados hacia el norte, y habitaciones y salas de estar con galerías, orientadas hacia el sur. Algunos pisos contienen salas de estar de doble altura. La parte oeste del edificio se desarrolla con una forma escalonada que genera terrazas privadas y cubiertas verdes con vistas.

Location: Paris, France
Building area:
2,560 m2 / 27,555 sq ft
Architecture team:
rh + architecture
Sustainability: RFR elements
General contractor:
Capaldi Construction
Photo credits: © Luc Boegly
Awards:
- BBC projects
organised by ADEME
and Region Ile-de-France
- « Prix grand public archicontemporaine des Maisons de l'architecture en France »

South facade

North facade

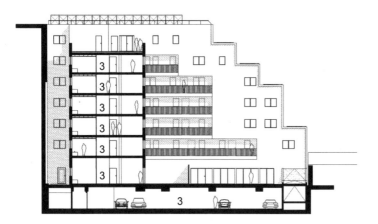

Longitudinal section

1. Nursery
2. Entry hall
3. Study
4. 2 rooms
5. 3 rooms
6. 4 rooms
7. Technical local
8. Parking
9. Courtyard

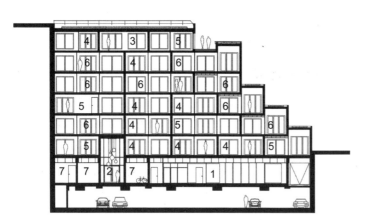

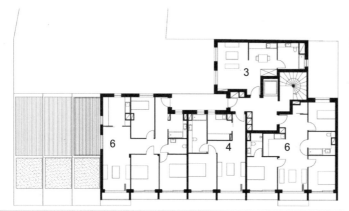

Fifth floor plan

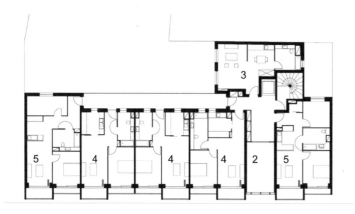

First floor plan

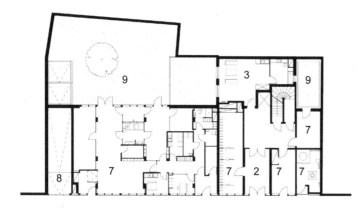

Ground floor plan

1. Nursery
2. Entry hall
3. Study
4. 2 rooms
5. 3 rooms
6. 4 rooms
7. Technical local
8. Parking
9. Courtyard

TONY OWEN PARTNERS

SOVEREIGN

Sylvania, Sydney, Australia
www.tonyowen.com.au

This set of 23 houses is situated on a sloping plot facing the river Georges. In order to provide privacy and optimise views and solar installations, a network of two-storey "L" shaped houses was designed on three levels leading down to the river. This L-shaped form generates central courtyards that create internal perspectives and maximise the sun in the bedrooms. The homes are stacked in such a way that the living rooms face a terrace on the roof of the lower unit. The interaction of the communal access roads, together with the use of topography and the definition of private spaces make the result resemble a small village. This sensation is reinforced by the use of a limited palette of materials that give homogeneity to the whole and add strength to the overall composition.

Este conjunto de 23 casas se sitúa en una parcela en pendiente orientada hacia el río Georges. Para proporcionar privacidad y optimizar las vistas y las instalaciones solares, se proyectó un entramado de casas de dos plantas en forma de "L" dispuestas en tres niveles que bajan hacia el río. Esta forma en "L" genera patios centrales que crean perspectivas internas y maximizan el sol en los dormitorios. Las viviendas se apilan de tal manera que las salas de estar se orientan hacia una terraza situada en el techo de la unidad inferior. La interacción de los caminos comunales de acceso, junto al uso de la topografía y la definición de los espacios privados hacen que el resultado se asemeje a un pequeño pueblo. Esta sensación se refuerza mediante el uso de una limitada paleta de materiales que dan homogeneidad al conjunto y agregan fuerza a la composición global.

Location: Sydney Australia
Building area: 3,450m2
Project team:
Tony Owen, Wendy Tong, Terry Leung, Byan Li.
Developer: QY Hansen
Structural engineer: Meinhardt
Services engineer: Erbas Consulting
Landscape consultant: John Locke Associates
Photo credits: © John Gollings

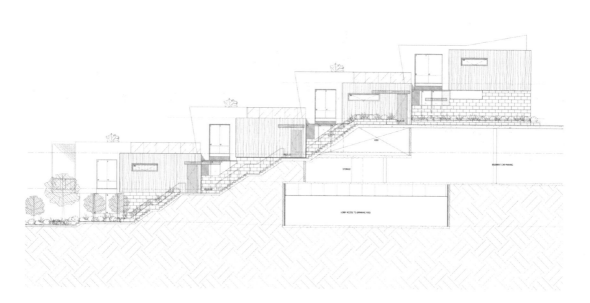

Site plan

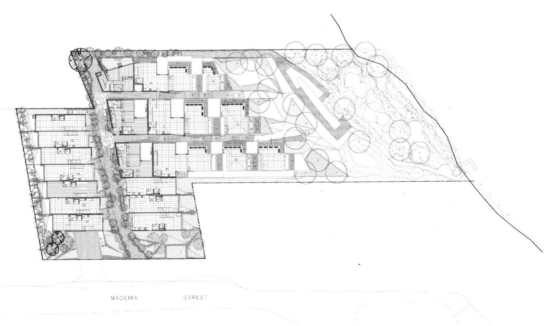

MADEIRA STREET

West elevation

BIG-BJARKE INGELS GROUP
DORTHEAVEJ RESIDENCE
Copenhagen, Denmark
www.big.dk

The project consists of 66 affordable housing born in collaboration with the non-profit association Lejerbo. The building represents a 5-storey porous wall that meanders around warehouses and industrial buildings and gently curves in its centre, creating a public square towards the street on the south side and a more enclosed green area to the north. The construction system is based on a checkered pattern formed by repetition and stacking of the accommodation modules, which creates a small terrace for each dwelling and gives depth to the south façade. The materials used are simple, with predominant use of wood and concrete in light tones. The façades are clad with long wooden planks that underline the structure of the building modules and alternate their direction to highlight the checkered pattern.

El proyecto consta de 66 viviendas asequibles y nace de la colaboración con la asociación sin ánimo de lucro Lejerbo. El edificio representa un muro poroso de 5 plantas de altura que serpentea en un entorno de almacenes y edificios industriales y que se curva suavemente en su centro, creando una plaza pública hacia la calle en el lado sur y una zona verde más cerrada hacia el norte. El sistema constructivo se basa en un patrón a cuadros formado por la repetición y el apilamiento de los módulos de alojamiento, que crea una pequeña terraza para cada vivienda y da profundidad a la fachada sur. Los materiales utilizados son sencillos, con uso predominante de la madera y el hormigón en tonos claros. Las fachadas se revisten con largos tablones de madera que subrayan la estructura de módulos del edificio y que alternan su dirección para resaltar el patrón a cuadros.

Size: 6,800 m2
Project type: Commission
Client: LEJERBO
Collaborators: MOE
Location text: Copenhagen, DK
Awards: Danish Architect Associations Lille Arne Award,
Partners in Charge: Bjarke Ingels, Finn Nørkjær
Project managers: Ole Elkjær-Larsen, Per Bo Madsen
Photo credits: © Rasmus Hjortshoj

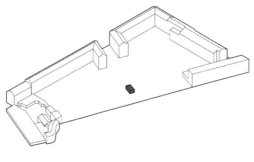

MODULE. The project is generated from a simple prefab structure.

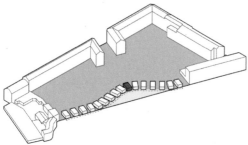

CURVE. The element is repeated along a curve. The system defines a courtyard for the urban block and introduces a public square towards the street.

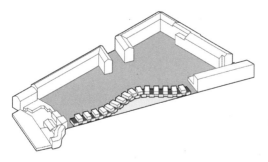

STARK. The element is stacked along the curve creating interstitial spaces that face yard and square.

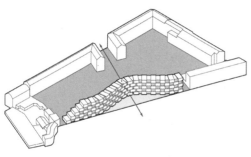

POROSITY. The building is raised to the height of the surroundings. A passage at the ground level allows public flow between square and yard.

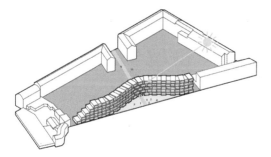

SOCIAL REALM. The system combines a valuable public space with social housing units optimally oriented.

North elevation / East elevation

South elevations / West elevation

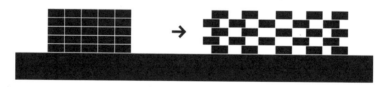

Concept diagram

Second floor plan

Ground floor plan

Sections

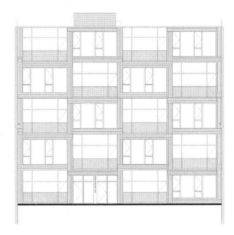

North elevation detail / South elevation detail

TRAMA ARQUITECTOS

CÍRCULO FRANCÉS

Guadalajara, Jalisco, México
www.trama.com.mx

The building is located in the Colonia Americana, one of the former neighborhoods that are reborn in the city, originally inhabited by the upper classes and later occupied by shops and offices. The project proposes the return of settlers to the area, trying not to promote an uncontrolled gentrification.

The building is divided into two blocks parallel to the streets that define the site and are opening from east to west. This layout, which enhances the trapezoidal shape of the site, creates an interior void that houses the nucleus of vertical communication and a communal space on the ground floor that contains the access to the dwellings and an urban garden.

The complex consists of a commercial ground floor, in front of which pleasant living spaces are developed. 60 dwellings of different types spread over the 6 upper floors.

El edificio se ubica en la Colonia Americana, una de las antiguas colonias que renacen en la ciudad, habitada en su origen por clases altas y posteriormente ocupada por comercios y oficinas. El proyecto plantea el retorno de pobladores a la zona, intentando no promover una gentrificación descontrolada.

Compositivamente, el edificio se desdobla en dos bloques paralelos a las calles que definen el solar y que se van abriendo de oriente a poniente. Esta disposición, que potencia la forma trapezoidal del solar, crea un vacío interior que aloja el núcleo de comunicación vertical y un espacio comunitario en planta baja que contiene el acceso a las viviendas y un huerto urbano.

El conjunto consta de unn planta baja comercial, frente a la que se desarrollan agradables espacios de convivencia, y 60 viviendas de diversas tipologías repartidas entre las 6 plantas superiores.

Name of the project: Círculo Francés
Location: López Cotilla #1223 corner with Atenas street, American colony, Guadalajara, Jalisco, Mexico
Built area: 16,800 m2
Architects authors of the work: Jaime Castiello Chávez, Héctor Santana, Edgardo Sandoval
Leading architects: Jorge I. Gutiérrez, Héctor Lozano Gray
Design team: Juan Carlos Barriga, Susana Cortés, Ana Castellanos, Salvador Hernández, Hugo Yáñez, Miguel A. Martínez
Project management: Emmanuel Calles and Gabriela González Lavalle
Structural calculation: Jorge Suárez M.
Electrical engineering: FMS Ingeniería
Hydrosanitary engineering: Hydrotechnics
Urban gardens: Nucleus Study, urban_cultivation deraiz
Landscaping: Between Plants
Photo credits / website: © Lorena Darquea

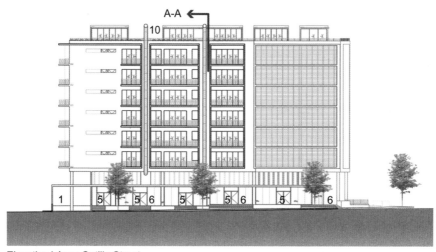

A-A ←

10

Elevation López Cotilla Street

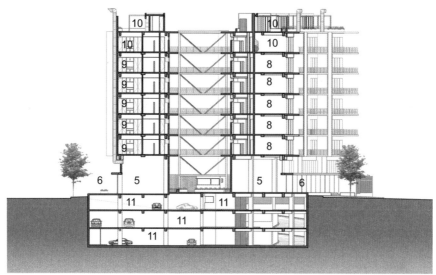

10
10
9
9
9
9
10
8
8
8
8

6
5
5
6

11
11
11
11

Section A-A

1. Parking entrance
2. Departments entrance
3. Surveillance booth
4. Urban orchard
5. Commercial
6. Commercial terrace
7. Services
8. Studio Department
9. 2 bedroom apartment
10. Penthouse
11. Underground parking

Sketch

Sketch

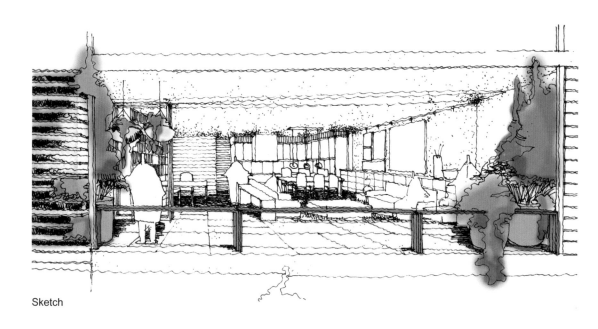

Sketch

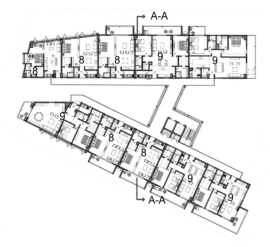

1 -5 levels

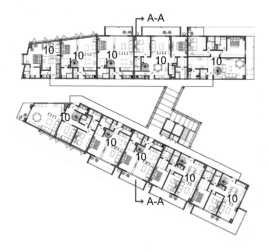

Level 6

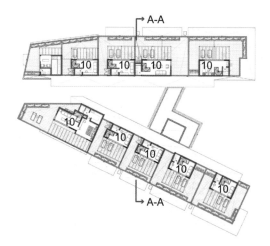

Level 7

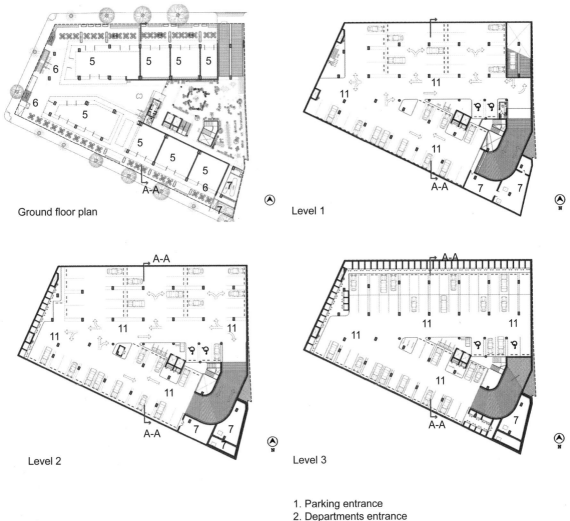

Ground floor plan

Level 1

Level 2

Level 3

1. Parking entrance
2. Departments entrance
3. Surveillance booth
4. Urban orchard
5. Commercial
6. Commercial terrace
7. Services
8. Studio Department
9. 2 bedroom apartment
10. Penthouse
11. Underground parking

VALERIE SCHWEITZER ARCHITECTS

THE TIDES BRENTWOOD

Los Angeles, California, USA
www.schweitzerarchitecture.com

The main objective in designing this five-story building was to enhance the neighborhood and celebrate the iconoclastic spirit of Los Angeles. Located in an interstitial area, the project promotes through the design of its façades a sense of place that pools ecological elements of the area, such as the Pacific Ocean, the predominant sun and the high palms that surround the site. Its exterior facade builds a dynamic connection with street life through elements such as large balconies that expand the interior through large windows. The façades include a pictorial component reflected in the Mondrian-inspired cavities that scale the vertical transportation cores, clad in grey stucco. Colour is used throughout the building not only as a cladding, but also as an architectural element that helps to sculpt the space.

El objetivo principal al diseñar este edificio de cinco plantas fue atraer al vecindario y celebrar el espíritu iconoclasta de Los Ángeles. Situado en un área intersticial, el proyecto promueve a través del diseño de sus fachadas una sensación de lugar que aglutina elementos ecológicos de la zona, como el Océano Pacífico, el sol predominante y las elevadas palmeras que rodean el lugar. Su imagen exterior construye una conexión dinámica con la vida de la calle mediante elementos como los amplios balcones que expanden el interior a través de grandes ventanales. Las fachadas incluyen un componente pictórico reflejado en las cavidades de inspiración Mondrian que escalan los núcleos de comunicación vertical revestidos de estuco gris. El color es utilizado en todo el edificio no sólo como revestimiento, sino como un elemento arquitectónico que ayuda a esculpir el espacio.

Location: 1157 South Bundy Drive, Los Angeles, CA
Design architect: Valerie Schweitzer AIA
of Valerie Schweitzer Architects—NYC, New York
Architect of record: Plus Architects, Los Angeles, CA
GC and construction manager: Kennedy Construction (Seamus Kennedy and Bob Van Dyke)
Photo credits: © Dan Arnold Photography, LA, CA JWP Studio, LA, CA

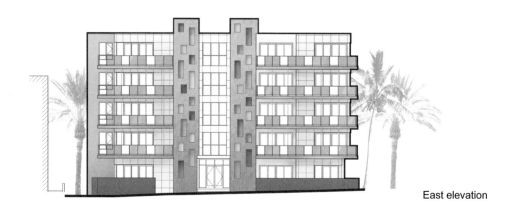

East elevation

North elevation

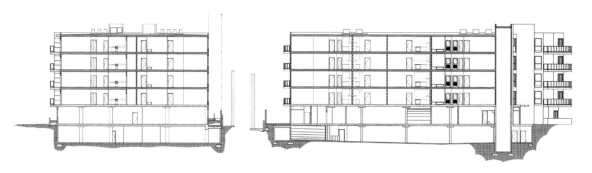

Cross section   Longitudinal section

113

GOSHEN AVENUE

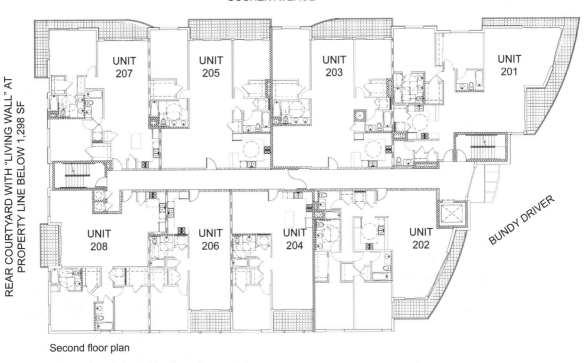

REAR COURTYARD WITH "LIVING WALL" AT
PROPERTY LINE BELOW 1,298 SF

UNIT 207

UNIT 205

UNIT 203

UNIT 201

UNIT 208

UNIT 206

UNIT 204

UNIT 202

BUNDY DRIVER

Second floor plan

YDS ARCHITECTS
VOID IN A FOREST
Tokyo, Japan
www.ydsaa.net

Located in the site next to a very large park, the concept is to take in abundant nature around the site and to create spaces people live feeling light and wind.
A court named 'Urban Garden' is put into the building to insert nature to daily life. The court functions as a square and is softly articulated by louvers from the forest around the site, it would mingle with nature. Stairs over the court functions as vibrant promenades which invoke fondness for nature. The stair and each corridor face the court and provide light and wind when one would come and go to their units, making it pleasant experiences. Through bay windows, one would see trees in the court as well as in the park and feel transitional changes by time and seasons.
At night, the court becomes shining garden with bamboo, providing extraordinary experiences for people with dark sky and wavering forests.

Situado en un terreno junto a un parque enorme, el concepto trata de acoger la abundante naturaleza que rodea el sitio y crear espacios donde la gente viva sintiendo la luz solar y el aire.
Un patio llamado «Jardín Urbano» se instala en el edificio para insertar la naturaleza en la vida cotidiana. Este patio funciona como una plaza y está suavemente articulado por medio de elementos del terreno, mezclándose con la naturaleza. Las escaleras del patio funcionan como pasajes vibrantes que invocan el cariño por la naturaleza. La escalera principal y cada uno de los pasillos proporcionan luz y aire, lo que convierte las experiencias en sensaciones agradables. A través de los ventanales se pueden ver los árboles tanto del porche como del parque y sentir los cambios del tiempo y las estaciones.
Por la noche, el espacio se convierte en un brillante jardín de bambú, proporcionando experiencias extraordinarias.

Location: Tokyo, Japan
Building area:
1,420 m2 / 15,285 sq ft
Architecture team:
Yoshitaka Uchino, Mana Muraki / YDS Architects
Collaborators:
Toshi Kozo Structural Design
Photo credits: © YDS Architects

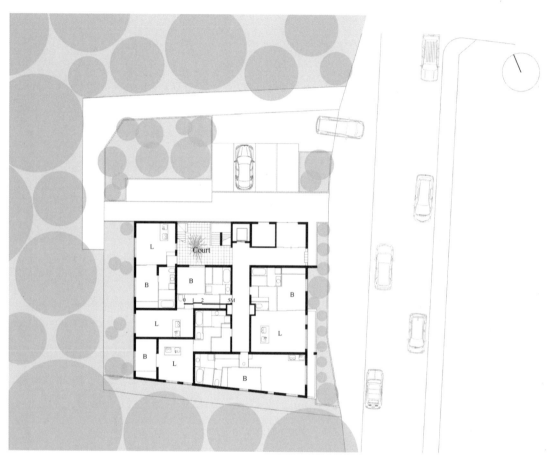

First floor plan

Concept diagrams

Fifth floor plan

Fourth floor plan

Third floor plan

Second floor plan

ATTIKA ARCHITEKTEN

LIVING ABOVE WATER

Zeeburgerbaai, Amsterdam
www.attika.nl

The public platforms offer panoramic views over the water and a fishing bench at the end.
The dark grey aluminium skin, which mimics the Dutch water, contrasts sharply with the beautiful colour accents and the glass of the windows. In this way, it is not so much the individual house that is emphasised, but the entire project as a whole. This provides a sharp contrast with the individual homes in the country's self-construction streets.
Residents' requirements, including roof terraces and extra space, have ensured that each house is made to measure and has a slightly different form.

Estas plataformas públicas situadas en el lago IJmeer en Amsterdam ofrecen vistas panorámicas del agua.
El aluminio gris oscuro, que imita el agua holandesa, contrasta fuertemente con los hermosos colores y el vidrio de las ventanas. De esta forma, no es tanto la casa individual lo que se enfatiza, sino todo el proyecto en su conjunto. Esto proporciona un marcado contraste con las viviendas individuales en las calles de autoconstrucción del país.
Los requisitos de los residentes, incluidas las terrazas en la azotea y el espacio adicional, han consistido en que cada casa esté hecha a medida y tenga una forma ligeramente diferente.

Location: Zeeburgerbaai, Amsterdam
Architecture team: Attika Architekten
Photo credits: © Bart van Hoek, Croce & Wir/ PREFA

3D image - bird's eye view

3D image - eye level

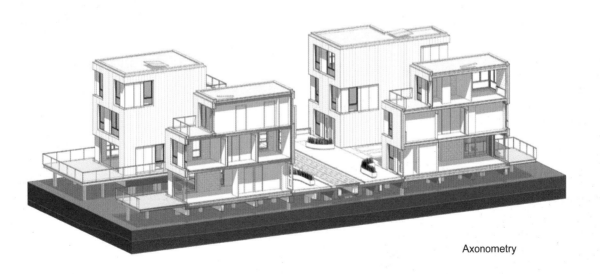

Axonometry

North west elevation. Patform 1

South east elevation. Patform 1

South west elevation. Patform 1

North west elevation. Patform 1

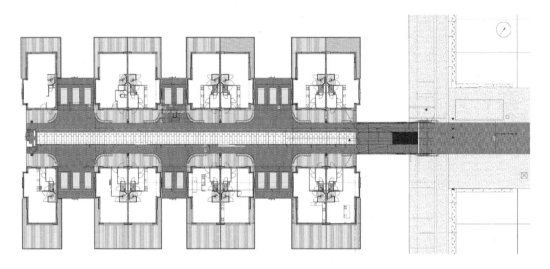

Floor plan

Sketch

ZECC GROUNDED ARCHITECTURE
TOWER APARTMENTS MEYSTER'S BUITEN
Utrecht, Nederland
www.zecc.nl

The Tower Apartments are the final part of an area transformation along the Merwede Canal in the Oog in Al district in Utrecht. Here was the Cereol factory where soy products for cattle feed were produced. Where the tower apartments now stand, there used to be large round silos for the storage of soy. The new residential tower is a direct reference to these silos. Like the former silo, the tower has a metal facade and the building is placed on a heavy concrete construction. The tight round shape of the silos has evolved into a freer formal language with large, fanned-out balconies.

The building is seen as an icon for the city and is an anchor point in the area. An unmistakably expressionist structure with a strong historical anchorage. Solitary and connected at the same time.

"The Tower Apartments" son la parte final de una transformación de un área del Canal Merwede en el distrito de Oog in Al en Utrecht. Aquí estaba la fábrica de Cereol donde se producían productos de soja para la alimentación del ganado.

Donde ahora se encuentran los apartamentos de la torre, solía haber grandes silos redondos para el almacenamiento de soja. La nueva torre residencial es una referencia directa a estos silos. Al igual que el antiguo silo, la torre tiene una fachada metálica y el edificio está colocado sobre una pesada construcción de hormigón. La forma redonda y ajustada de los silos se ha convertido en un estilo formal más libre con balcones grandes en abanico.

El edificio se ha convertido en un ícono de la ciudad, y es un punto de anclaje en el área. Una estructura inconfundiblemente expresionista con un fuerte anclaje histórico. Solitario y conectado al mismo tiempo.

Location: Utrecht, Nederland
Architecture team: Zecc Grounded Architecture
Photo credits: © Stijnstijl fotografie

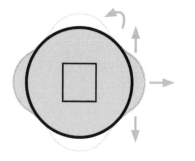

Concept diagram
Free categorization light
3-sided view expression
Dynamics little floor space
Privacy
Large outdoor area

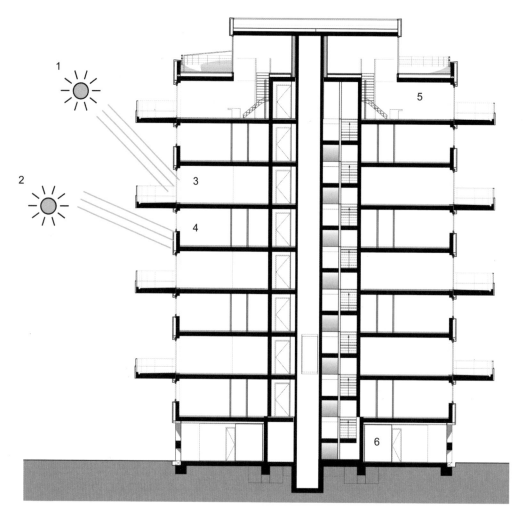

Section

1. Summer
2. Winter
3. Living
4. Bedroom
5. Penthouses
6. V column
7. Entry/storage

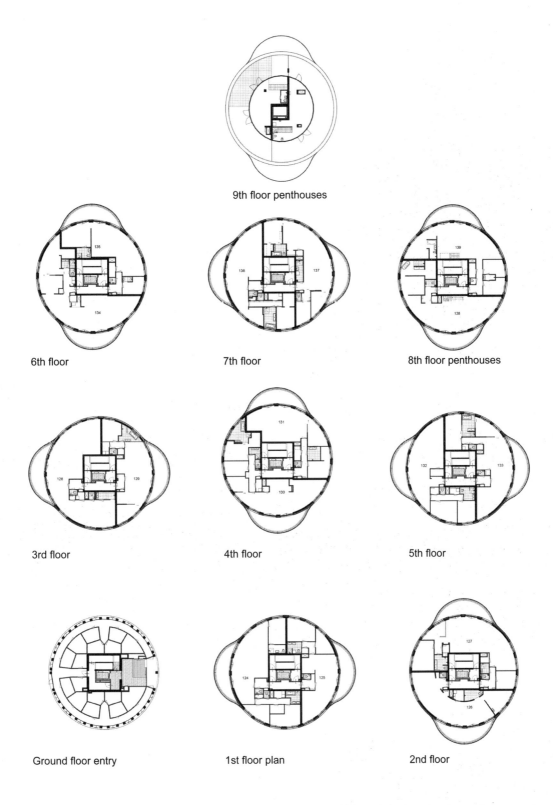

9th floor penthouses

6th floor

7th floor

8th floor penthouses

3rd floor

4th floor

5th floor

Ground floor entry

1st floor plan

2nd floor